LIFE
TO THE POWER OF
NOTHING

David Turner

Rock's Mills Press
Oakville, Ontario
2019

Published by

Rock's Mills Press

www.rocksmillspress.com

Cover design: Liam Turner-Ponomareff

For information, please contact Rock's Mills Press at
customer.service@rocksmillspress.com

"Wiyaw"
"Greetings" (in Nunggubuyu)

from Jabeni and Xavier of the Warnungamadada,
pending Xavier's initiation at Numbulwar
(courtesy of Jenny Baird)

Contents

Preface

It was fifty years ago in February of 1969 that my wife Ruth and I first set foot on a remote island in north Australia to research the way of life of the local Aboriginal people, just as mining was commencing on their land—a couple from Canada via London, England, and Perth, Western Australia, myself enrolled as a Ph.D. student at the University of Western Australia, sent to Groote Eylandt in the Northern Territory by my professor, Ronald M. Berndt.

A tent in the middle of the Aboriginal camp at Angurugu for daytime work (the photo below shows Ruth with Peter Wurramara), a "staging house" across the Angurugu River as living quarters: spiders, snakes, a river to cross every evening with the risk of salt-water crocs swimming upstream. A wet season that's too wet and hot, a dry season that's too dry and hot, infection from even the slightest cut. Trying to learn Anindilyaugwa, one of the most complex languages in the world. Missionaries, mining. The whole gamut.

All this time, all those revisits in between, articles and books published, working to come to an understanding of what makes these Ab-

original people and their way of life tick. But what better way to understand something than to become part of it yourself? And what better way to express a basic understanding than in just a few words, leaving the rest to the readers' experiences in their own environment? After all, we're all the same kind of people. Aren't we? Capable of the same experiences. Hopefully.

There was continuity in my experience of their world until the beginning of this century when my situation changed dramatically: a child, a detour to the Arctic, the death of my mentor, Nagulaba:na (Gula) Lalara. So, for 16 years all that knowledge and experience has lain dormant apart from keeping in touch with Jabeni through Jenny in Darwin. Jenny was married to Warren, Jabeni's *na:nigama* (in our terms, "younger brother," but much more and less in theirs). Then circumstances arose I could not ignore and all of a sudden it rushed to the surface, all bundled up in a quite compact and summary form. It had been integrating itself without my help all this time.

Professor Berndt once said that he thought Aborigines had seen signs of Divine Intent in the world and acted upon them. With all due respect, I agree that they saw signs of intent in the world from somewhere, but I don't think they emanated from a Divinity.

I. THE COSMOS

The Cosmos is like a vast cloud. Here and there you can see different patches of light and shade and almost make out recognizable shapes and forms. The rain is falling in a mist, here and there from different parts of the cloud, the drops splashing into the ocean below, each droplet creating an impression, becoming an incarnation. Waves roll across the ocean connecting all the "places" in the water where each droplet has made an impression and become some*thing*. Finally the sun peeks through the mist and the waters begin to evaporate, drawing the droplets from their respective "places" back up into the sky to re-form the cloud and the cycle continues.

The vast cloud is Amawurrena,[1] the "stuff of original creation," on the "other side."

The patches of light and shade, forces for forming.

The mist, the "stuff of original creation" on "this side."

The droplets, the givers of life,

The impression each drop makes in the waters, a mould,

Each drop, a material incarnation.

Within certain incarnations, a vital spirit.

Connections between the moulds, activated by the power of Amawurrena.

Waves f(F)orm, travel through, connecting part of one to the other.

anti-thesis--->thesis===>plurality=**II**

Nothingness--->being===>relationship

The power, the proclivity, to give—*yugwa*

Of yourself to others, of the things you have that they lack.

Its most intimate expression, *lyelyingmina*, love.

In tension with the proclivity to take.

To yourself from others, of the things they have that you want.

thesis--->anti-thesis===>synthesis=**I**

something--->opposed by something else===>resolved into unity

or one destroys the other

Its most intimate expression, hate.

The basis of this vision of the Cosmos is not so much the imagination as experience.

---

1. If small-n "nothing" is *nar'a:bina*, literally "no-thing"—the absence of things—then capital N-nothing is Amawurrena—what remains in the absence of things.

Laughing Waves

The term is *megamainggamandja* and it appeared again and again in the Wurramara's Songs of Yabongwa, the Rainbow Serpent(s)—multiple manifestations of which co-exist at the same "out-of-time." The Wurramara are the Aboriginal people of Amara, central Amagalyuagba, Bickerton Island, adjacent to Groote Eylandt. The term was translated for me as "the waves are laughing, the waves are laughing." This was a bit of a puzzle and had always stuck in my mind. How could waves "laugh"? So in 1986 on a return visit I asked Murabuda Wurramarrba (they-of-the-two-points-on-either-side-of-South-Bay-on-Bickerton) about it. He replied, not with an explanation, but with an instruction: if you go down to the sea in the dry season in the afternoon when the south-east wind (Mamariga) is blowing its strongest and the tide is coming in and look out over the open water you will see what we see and understand how waves could laugh.

The appropriate circumstances materialized late one afternoon while I was out on Bickerton. I borrowed a four-wheel drive and drove across to one of my favourite places, A:nemurremadja, on the south-east corner of the island, looking across the Gulf of Carpentaria to Groote Eylandt. I parked the vehicle and set off on foot over the dunes to the beach and looked out over the wide expanse of the Gulf. As I walked down off the dunes and on to the beach I looked up at the sea. The waves were laughing. I don't know how to explain it, but they were. The whole sea was alive. It was like looking at a million waves arranged within a grid, each precisely the same, each with the same wisp of whitecap spitting from its peak, each chuckling away to itself. The impression was of something alive and in motion which was at the same time at rest. I became overwhelmed by a sense of Form—an illumination—over and above each individual wave itself.

What I saw was waveForm(s) through which waves of water appeared to be flowing, one to the other. I just sat there on the beach chuckling away to myself—laughing with the waves.

*   *   *

The experience had five levels, one implicit. First was the experience of water—matter—itself, the second the perception of waves as such, and the third of waves replicated as a discernible form. The fourth stage was the perception of the Form of each wave on another plane of existence over and above the water itself. Add to this scene of waveForms the dynamic of "spitting" as the Aborigines call it—the wisp of whitecap on each wave suggestive of force and motion—and the more discriminating impression was not of water—matter—passing though waveForms, as of waveForms *expelling* bits of matter one to the other. (A fifth and final stage could be the Form of those Forms, a singleness of Form that defined each and every wave as a wave, but this would be my intellectual imposition on the scene—a projection beyond the scene, not something I actually saw—what we can term the monist mistake).

Megamainggamandja may seem to be a metaphor but it has a very real basis in experience in the sense of locating an experience that connects you to the world around you in a profound way. What I saw here, and Aborigines see in many other contexts, is not a "belief" based on faith, but a mode of perception. The Aborigines have penetrated the world of appearances in order to reach a deeper level of understanding which, in the final analysis, is beyond the grasp of analysis and connects the whole human enterprise into, well, the Cosmos.

* * *

The activating, transforming, power of Amawurrena manifests itself as *awarrawalya*, an "enveloping lightness of being," around all animate and inanimate objects that in turn marks their Essence of Being or Form. Awarrawalya *visually* identifies things as a certain *kind* (animal, plant, human, object, including the different kinds of each), as distinct from a taxonomic classification (which is also featured). Awarrawalya is also the term for shadow, "a reverse projection of an object," as well as for the bark huts that house the various Angalya (below), in sacred ceremonies such as Mardaiya:n.

Amawurrena, all bundled up and concentrated, constitutes an animating force, or vital spirit, within all living things which the Aborigines term *amugwa* (which, together with Amawurrena and *awarrawalya*, are referred to as *alawuduwarra*, the sacred). The *amugwa* is not something we are able to see—not while it is within ourselves at least—but are able to *feel* as a "quickening or enlivening"—what I felt during my experience of laughing waves. It is expressed metaphorically in such terms as *augwungwa amugwa*, "the gushingness of the water," or *angwura amugwa*, "the glowingness of the coals," of a fire.

When the body dies the *amugwa* is released to separate from its enfolding *awarrawalya* to pass to the "other side" and reconnect with Amawurrena, the "stuff" of original creation. The "mould" then "evaporates" and follows. But, in a sense, this is not the end of "you" here. As we proceed through life something of the Amawurrena of the *awarrawalya* of yourself is left behind or "rubs off" on the people and things around you and connects us to each other and to nature whether we are consciously aware of it or not. This is to blur the distinction between "me" and "you"— "us" and "them"— "we" and "it"—and renders us, at the most basic level, part of one in the other, again, whether we are aware of it or not.

So where does this overall realization lead us?

If we are essentially this "stuff of original creation," Formed into entities predisposed to give rather than receive, then we should go with the flow rather than against it and do so at all levels in our lives in relation to others and to nature, taking only what she is willing to give and nurturing her in the meantime. If we are truly a part of one another in this subtle and abiding sense, then just Who am "I"? Who are "They"? What is "It"? Certainly not writ in the singular.

*　　*　　*

The archaeological evidence suggests the Aborigines inhabited the Australian continent for some 70,000 years without organized warfare for the purpose of appropriating territory and exterminating others. As Scott Cane puts it in *First Footprints: The Epic Story of the First Australians* (Allen & Unwin, 2013), commenting on Aboriginal rock art, what we have here is "an ancient society of image-makers" whose visions carried with them "an implication of great social concord" suggesting "social coherence and communication on a scale that spans the continent."

Art

The images portrayed by Aboriginal artists are, by and large, of Songs, which in turn locate Essences of Being. These are the "Amawurrena of *awarrawalya*," of such real-world phenomena as stingrays, sharks, sawfishes, and natural formations, and which allow us to visually define them as a certain *kind* of thing as mentioned above.

In the painting on the next page by Djabargwa Wurrabadelamba, "Yingwa, Crow, with Bara, the West Wind," the Crow we see is obviously not an ordinary crow. There's "something about" it—balance and proportion—that transcends the appearance of a real crow and it is highlighted by the red outline-line symbolizing the Amawurrena of *awarrawalya,* or Essence of Being, of the subject, that is, its Form. But what about Bara? How do you represent the Essence of Being or Form of a wind?

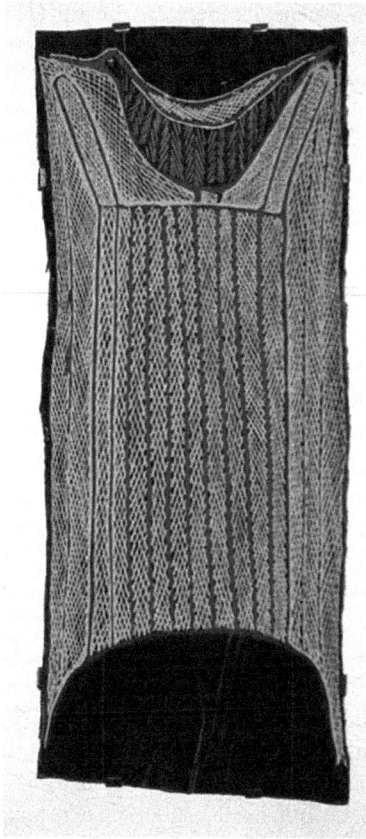

The larger image is actually a pretty accurate depiction of the sail of a Macassan ship or prau. The Macassans were seasonal visitors from Indonesia before the advent of Europeans. They arrived on the west wind with the rainy season and left on the east wind with the dry. This image is symbolic of that association. The inset image is an ancient representation of the West Wind found in cave paintings on Groote Eylandt. It is a more formal representation but with one feature coming close to being a "something about" the West Wind without actually being the wind. These are the two prongs extending from the top of the main body of the image. The extensions are the "something about" that is the buildup of the clouds on the horizon as a prelude to the appearance of the rainy season when the prevailing winds begin to blow from the west. They are described in everyday speech and in Song as *nuwardja:aiya:ba*, "the clouds are standing up, the clouds are standing up."

There are five dimensions depicted in art: (1) the medium itself (bark); (2) the depiction of a real life scene such as people fishing or hunting, without infilling; (3) the depiction of the Amawurrena of *awarrawalya*, or Essence of Being of a subject represented by the outline line; (4) infilling as a patterning of lines indicating this subject is on the "other side," that is, sacred rather than secular; (5) the solid or sometimes blank background, representing Amawurrena as such, the "stuff of original creation."

Music

Here, five dimensions are also involved:

Level 1: instruments—tapping sticks (*alyingba*), didjeridu (*yiraga*), and voice (*yengbina*). These add meaning to the voice in performance and you have what is termed your Ama:ba or Song.

Level 2: sound—sets the stage. The sticks announce "we are coming over" and act as a kind of sonic sound-bridge opening up a channel to the "other side," then the drone of the *yiraga* follows, channeling the player's *amugwa* across on his breath, followed by the voice on the breath of the singer which channels his or her *amugwa*.

Level 3: words—establish meaning on two levels: each word as such and the activities they describe when strung together as a Song. However, deciphering this meaning from these words is no easy task, which makes following the events they relate even harder. These are particular humans, animals, and natural formations appearing in Essence of Being Form travelling on the "other side," stopping here and there, creating impressions, inducing material incarnations, moving on and on ... repeat, repeat, repeat. What they *actually* are is extremely complex. One interpretation, given by Aborigines themselves, is that these are the original Creation Beings active *aragaragbagiyawiya*, or a long, long, time ago, responsible for incarnating the world as we know it. Another interpretation, also given by the Aborigines themselves, is that these Beings are here and now but *alawuduwarra*, or on the "other side." My take, as we'll see later, is that they are there to make a point. Whatever they "really" are, figuring out what is being sung about them during a performance, unless you are the singer, is nigh on impossible:

The Songman or woman may be singing Wurrawuminya, Black Duck, for instance, but the same term could also refer to Grey Teal, Water Whistling Duck, Grass Whiteline Duck, Green Pygmy Goose, or Little Grebe. Meaning depends on context and this the Songman or woman controls. For example, Dove and Spider are both Derraragugwa. But the new name for Spider is Dagwarargwa, which literally means Thread and refs to the weave in a piece of cloth, Dumbala. Dumbala takes us to Sail and hence to Ship. Thread is like Ma:rra, String, and String is what what Dove pulled around on her journey. But it wasn't really String, it was a piece of Wurrumilya:lya or Burney Vine. Wurrumilya:lya comes under Spider because Spider Webs are like Clusters of Vines. Yimurralya or Green Ants come in under Spider because Vines are where you find them. Spider Webs are like the Weave in a Piece of Cloth, are made of Threads, are like the piece of Vine pulled by Dove which is what Ship was pulled with. Dove String broke just like Ship Rope broke and at the same place.

Like I said, you try and figure out what is being sung!

Level 4: melodic contour—the sound-shape of the Song is its melodic contour and is a clue as to its identity. But, again, only a clue, as the same melodic contour can refer to different subjects and different subjects can have the same melodic contour. For example, Na:engmenara's Song for Mamariga or East Wind begins on a high note then undulates its way steadily down toward a low note. But then so does Gula's tune for the Angurugu River. Badjura's Song for Mamariga or East Wind begins on a low note then undulates in a regular pattern to the end. But so does Nawanma's Song for Wururwa:ba or Parrot. Both Gula's Song for Alumera, Silt-Churned-up-by-Stingray, and A:berigba, Reef, begin on a mid-point note and undulate down to a low note.

Level 5: Rhythm ratio—the number of beats per measure of the tapping sticks in relation to the number of beats of the *yiraga* in relation to the number of beats of the singing itself. Bara, or West Wind, Songs of the Warnungwadarrbalanga, for instance, favour a 6:3:1 rhythm ratio; Mabilya or Dirty Tide Songs, 6:2:1; Maraugwa or Sea Fan Songs, 3:3:1; Dermala or North (east) Wind Songs 4:2:1. The Warnungwamalangwa's Da:nunggulangwa, or Porpoise Songs are 2:1:1 and so on.

This level identifies the true meaning of what is being sung (e.g. Black Duck and not Grey Teal), a "secret" first noted by Catherine Ellis in *Aboriginal Music* (University of Queensland Press, 1985) in relation to Pitjantjantjara music in Central Australia where only sticks and voice are employed. We are now at the level of mathematics, and as far as we can go. If you are your Song and your Song is ultimately a mathematical formula, then what this is sounding you loud and clear is that in the final analysis you "really" are *No*thing at all (and probably explains why Catherine Ellis got in trouble with the Pitjantjantajara for revealing their rhythm-ratio secret in her book).

By level 5 in all domains, one confesses that ultimate understanding is beyond the reach of mere mortals. This is essentially what you learn in the final stage of initiation when the Essences of Beings of the subjects of your Songs on which you are named are revealed to you carved in absolute minimalist Form—as with rhythm-ratios, without substantial content—with the same implication that in the final analysis you are Nothing at all (on art and life, see *Afterlife Before Genesis: An Introduction—Accessing the Eternal through Australian Aboriginal Music* [Peter Lang Publishing, 1997]).

*　　*　　*

There is coherence between the way the Cosmos is experienced and the way it is represented in art and music. Why should it not surprise us that the institutions of peace, order and good government should cohere in the same manner?

Angalya

Members of an Angalya are connected by names selected from within a certain corpus of Songs connected to the Essences of Beings of certain animals, plants and natural formations. These are in one sense inherited *from* the previous generation insofar as they are present there and, in another sense, *on* your own generation insofar as they are dreamed *for* the child from within this corpus, usually *by* a child. Once known, the name or names are then sung to the birth-child by the *nungwa* or "father" in our terms but considered primarily as the "husband of the mother," or *na:ningya*, in theirs who, through prolonged relations with her, has opened up a passageway to allow for the entry of this *amugwa* into this world.

The physical aspect of the child-to-come is seen as made in the womb and is constituted of blood from the mother and bone from the husband. But this is not who the child *is*. The child is his or her name, or Alara, and name is Song. Any attempt to attribute a child's physical resemblance to *anyone* after he or she is born is regarded as a grave insult.

Your name may originate from the Essence of Being of a certain animal or natural formation such as Duwalya or Curlew, but no one is actually named on its Essence of Being *as such*. The Warnungamadada (they-of-Amadadi, Gula's and Jabeni's Angalya), for instance, sing Dangerous Snakes, but no one is named King Brown or Death Adder. But one person *is* named Naluggwibanga or Superfical-King-Brown-Snake-Bite. And another of his names is Nalungbayibonga, Deeper-King-Brown-Snake-Bite. To name on the Essence of Being as such would be to assign a unity to everyone as a group rather than part-of-one-in-the-otherness. (Surnames such as Lalara and Amagula designated for "everyone" in the

Angalya are an Australian government invention designed to facilitate record-keeping.)

Nenindilyaragwagwa's name is connected to Yimaduwaya or Stingray and means (take a deep breath) Silt-Churned-Up-By-the-Tide-Where-The-Fresh-Water-Flows-From-A-Creek-At-Armadadi-On-The-Mainland-And-Mixes-With-The-Sea-And-Is-Gone-Forever-Never--Turning-Back.

If your Song bestows membership in the Angalya, then membership in the Angalya bestows on you a kind of citizenship which you carry around with you like a passport in the form of your Song. This affords you *primary* jurisdiction over "your" places—those mentioned in your Song—and *secondary* jurisdiction over those other places mentioned in Songs belonging to others but in association with the same Essence of Being. All people and places connected in this way define the boundaries of Angalya.

These Angalya-places, then, are those from which you can leave and return at your leisure, knowing your rights there are secure despite your absence—so long as you respect the rights of others elsewhere with *different* Songs from your own. Those in Angalya elsewhere with Songs whose subjects' activities overlap with yours are obliged to afford you tertiary right there, as are you with respect to them in turn.

As you might expect in a way of life where "land rights" are assigned on an "abstract-eternal" basis, what is an anathema here is the assertion of rights by simple residence or occupation. This brings us to Nambirrirrma.

*   *   *

In 1969 Galiyawa of the Wurramarrba, then in his eighties, told me the story of a fellow named Nambirrirrma Na:nagbarrnga, "he who sits down."

A man appears from nowhere out of a cloud on the rain to two men out fishing along the beach of South Bay on Bickerton Island, one of whom is Wurramarrba, the other Warnungwadarrbalangwa whose country is along the west coast of the island. Nambirrirrma lands, stands up, and then sits down, as first one of the witnesses approaches and then the other. Nambirrirrma claims to be Wurramara in whose country he has just landed. But he is described by the Wurramarrba witness as a "different kind of man," and appears to have no prior connections either here or on the mainland so far as they can tell, though he does speak their language which is a bit of a mystery. The two witnesses try and persuade him to travel across the island to the east coast to fetch the Wurramara people who are visiting their mother's people, the Wurra:nggilyangba, there, but he refuses and continues to "sit down" where he is. So the Wurramarrba witness goes instead, and the other witness leaves to fetch his own people on the west coast. Nambirrirrma stays put. When they all return, they negotiate their relationship to him by laying down the rules of descent and marriage as if he is Wurramara, pointing out where certain people properly belong, and assign him a wife (the ideal here is to marry the same unrelated-in-Song Angalya every second generation). Nambirrirrma and his wife have a child who later dies. Nambirrirrma dies. End of story.

What's significant about Nambirrirrma is that he claims to be Wurramara but has no name or spiritual identity in terms of a Song, Wurramara's or otherwise. He defines himself simply as "he who sits down." This would appear to be rather risky amongst a people where territorial rights by virtue of simple residence are heresy!

Nambirrirrma is the Aborigines' collective *antithesis*. Why didn't they just kill him and have done with it? Well, because they are in *plurality mode* (see below, pp. 28–29). The stranger has *No* place so they are moved to afford him one. They even appear to validate his status by further integrating him into their society. But, relax, the status quo is reaffirmed: Nambirrirrma dies and the principle he represents dies with him. And with that ends the "threat" of rights by simple residence.

Did it really happen? Or is it just a story to illustrate a point? Could be both. But there is a certain "experimental" logic to the tale that points in the latter direction and has broader implications beyond this story: start by imagining something that is the opposite to the status quo in your world, insert it into that world, and then think through the probable consequences. Disastrous? Then try and minimize the threat by weakening it through some kind of imagined mediation. When that appears to fail, simply deny the problem, hoping it will simply disappear.

opposition (threat)---->weakening---->mediation====> illusion of solution

The statement of opposition in the Nambirrirrma tale is "rights by virtue of simple residence"; the weakener, summoning people from the island's Angalya and instructing Nambirrirrma in the rules of relationship; the mediation, providing him with a wife; the illusion of a solution, having him simply die off. Illusory because others like him could still appear "out of the blue" from nowhere and they could do nothing about it.

The story of Yandarranga, Central Hill, works through a similar issue: the potential threat to the way of life of "sitting down" for too long in some else's Angalya and, in this case, almost getting involved in an inappropriate relationship.

Central Hill begins his journey in Central Arnhem Land in the lands of the Nemamurdudi then moves eastward to the lands of the Ngalmi where he "sits down." But it is too dirty so he moves on to Warnungamadada county on the coast. Here he keeps sinking down in the mud so he moves out into the Gulf of Carpentaria and across to Bickerton landing at another Warnungamadada place there. Then he cuts across land to arrive in the country of the Wurra:nggilyangba where he "throws out his anchor" and lands. But as he is drying himself off, he finds himself sinking down in the mud again so he "throws off some 'sons'" and begins to move on, discarding some Wild Apples along the way. This is where he meets the blind woman Dimimba and helps her dig up some yams. But he sinks down in the mud to the point where he can barely drag himself along but manages to make it to the coast and heads for Groote Eylandt oblivious to the fact that Dimimba has gathered up her spear and spear-thrower and has hurled two spears at him from behind. But she misses—she's blind—and the two spears create two islands where they land. Grief-stricken and angry, Dimimba gashes herself in the head until blood flows, so much blood that it spills into the sea and flows all the way over to Groote Eylandt. Then she returns to her country with Central Hill's "sons." The "sons" eventually spread the Anindilyaugwa language everywhere.

Meanwhile Central Hill reaches Groote Eylandt in Warnungwudjaragba country but at a place belonging to the Warnungangwurugwerigba (a kind of "country within a country" for "guests" unrelated to you by Song). He begins to sink down again and throws off some more "sons" who tell him to leave this place and, "Go on to Warnungangwurugwerigba country," in central Groote Eylandt. So he did, sitting down there and making himself comfortable. Then he created Lake Hubert, an inland sea where he caught lots of fish.

There are two potential threats to the status quo at issue here. The first is that Central Hill sits down and begins to sink in the mud at various places on his journey. Should he do so to the point of immobility and actually create something there—impressing his Essence of Being—he would establish a right of primary jurisdiction and acquire a Song. But each time this threatens to happen, he manages to drag himself away—with help from his "sons"— until he reaches his final resting place.

So, instead of acquiring jurisdiction over all the places he visits and becoming a unifier, by moving on Central Hill becomes a connector and, in context of the logic of the tale, at once a potential threat and at the same time a weakener and a mediator. The illusion of a solution to this potential threat? Just keep on moving while temporarily staying put—by way of his "sons" whom he leaves behind to potentially "sink in" where they shouldn't to realize precisely what he has just managed to avoid. But they eventually move on to spread the Anindilyaugwa language "every-where," apparently without establishing a primary jurisdiction of their own.

In other words, "sinking in" to others' jurisdictions and others into yours is always a danger in Aboriginal society; or, rather, "singing in" to others' jurisdictions. To know your Songs is to know your Angalya in all its details but there is always the danger that someone will "land" in your Song from one of theirs if you don't maintain all these details in terms of the places and events recounted. New signs of cosmological intent can suddenly "appear" out of the blue in the environment connecting some-one else's Song to your own. If not challenged, it's "theirs" in an Aborig-inal kind of way. Masking your Songs with multiple meanings to "fool" others as to what you are really singing is a way of protecting against this. If they don't know your Song, they can't sing in, by mistake or otherwise.

The second potential threat to the status quo in the Central Hill tale, of course, is Dimimba, not only because she almost succeeds in "grounding" him, but also because she engages in an anomalous work-ing relationship: in the Aboriginal way of life, men hunt, women gather, particularly in a domestic context, though there are exceptions such as when one is alone in the bush and in need of food. In the tale the man gathers with a woman in a co-production relationship. Their relationship may potentially be even more anomalous than this as we are not told if Dimimba is Warra:nggilyanba and belongs to this place or whether she has married in from another Angalya. Warra:nggilyanba and War-nungangwurugwerigba have intersecting Songs and are forbidden to marry. Her response to him leaving and the fact that she takes his "sons" indicates she wants him as a husband, which could be forbidden. Herein lies the potentially disastrous consequence of "sitting down" in the wrong place for too long, which the "citizens" in the Nambirrirrma tale manage to avoid by assigning him a appropriate wife.

* * *

Our acceptance of these tales as something Aboriginal people believe actually happened falls easily into our biases. "They" think magically to explain things, "we" think scientifically. But what if the stories they relate are initially presented as "true" in order to gain inductees' attention, but at more advanced stages of initiation are gradually revealed to be problem-solving exercises—indeed logico-deductive exercises aimed at anticipating problems before they arise—and are not to be taken literally? How then do we interpret images from the past such as rock art and engravings? Real fighting depicted, or a teaching to illustrate the disastrous consequences of fighting should it happen?

* * *

Arumandja marks the place on Bickerton where Nambirrirrma "sat down" and where he and his "son" are buried. I was taken there in 1986 by Milurndurn Wurramara.

Through the lens of a camera the site looks pretty nondescript, just some shells in a depression in the ground, and there were no restric-

tions on taking a picture. But non-appearances can be illuminating. On a revisit in 1987 I invited John McLaren, a friend from Darwin, over to visit and thought it would be cool to show him where Nambirrirrma "sat down." So off we set from the outstation at Milya:gburra along the beach of South Bay. We got to about where I thought was the middle of the bay and turned inland just off the beach. I looked and looked around but nowhere was that shell midden to be found. So back to the beach we went, me feeling more than a little sheepish. I was just shuffling around looking nowhere in particular when I turned to look out at the bay. It was in a perfectly symmetrical "horseshoe" Form—not the actual bay, the water and the surrounding land as such—but a dimension over and above the actual bay itself, an illumination which seemed to bring all within its ken. I took it in for moment and then turned right around 180 degrees and walked off the beach back onto the grass. And there was the midden.

The midden/burial site was there for a reason and I had just experienced it. It was at a point of perfect symmetry which identified it as a sacred place connected to another dimension. Like my experience of "laughing waves," this one too had a number of levels: first, simply the experience of water and land as such, next the perception of water bounded by land as a partially enclosed space, then the enclosure itself as distinct form, followed the appearance of the bay as a perfectly symmetrical, illuminated, Form—level four.

*   *   *

The Bickerton natural environment lies basically unspoiled compared to Groote Eylandt as mining has been prohibited here and non-Aboriginal people forbidden from landing on its shores. It is here that the full power of Nothing can still be seen. I mean this in the sense of the power of the Angalya as an abstract-eternal jurisdiction (actually, a collection of individual, interrelated, ones) to "give." Each of the island's four jurisdictions encompasses an *abundance* of one particular resource which is sung—long yams in the Wurramarrba's, wild apples in the Wurra:ngilyangba's, best parrot fishing grounds in the Warnungwadarrbalangwa's, and the only permanent supply of fresh water gathered in rock soaks in the Wurramara's. Being sung renders them prohibited as food to those singing them. (But fresh water? This one had me stumped until I found out that what was prohibited were the plants and animals that inhabited fresh water, not the water itself). In a sense, then, the Angalya is "expelling" *all* of something it has to those in another Angalya who lack it and are in need—and on a consistent basis. Either the Angalya had to be positioned this way to achieve this or—recall Central Hill dropping off Wild Apples in Wurra:ngilyangba country on Bickerton—they were planted there. I was told that yams were sometimes transplanted from Bickerton to Groote Eylandt in the pre-European past.

I don't know about you the reader, but at the time I figured this out it blew me away and and it still does today when I look back at it.

It was impossible to test this out on Groote Eylandt as strip-mining had already taken its toll on the island's environment and, as for elsewhere, well, it's much the same story for this and other reasons in other parts of Australia, even where Aborigines are still living something of a traditional lifestyle. But there is another application of this principle on a personal level.

Gula told me that his mother's husband, Banjo (English), took his three sons aside at an early age and allocated a division of labour among them: Gula was to do the Ama:ba (Songs), Alan to do the *a:rriba:rriba* (bush, that is, fishing and hunting), and Jambana to deal with Wurra-balanda (Europeans). When I first arrived in 1969 that's what each of them did. In fact, each had become so adept at the task assigned that it is fair to say they were among the best at what they did in general. Alan was always out hunting and fishing, Jambana had reached the point in his dealings with Wurrabalanda that he was on the verge of organizing the few Aboriginal employees at the mining company into a union, and Gula.…

II. ACCESSING THE ETERNAL

To begin with, this is going to be the most difficult part of this narrative for many of you to accept. It is about accessing and utilizing that invisible realm that constitutes the Amawurrena of *awarrawalya* and *amugwa*. But those recounting their experiences of this to me are neither charlatans nor frauds. They relate them to each other as everyday matters as if they were, say, going fishing. In fact, the two kinds of experiences are often intertwined, such as when I was fishing with Gula and saw and heard him singing fish to his hook while mine, with me standing just a few metres away armed with bait, remained forever empty. Aboriginal people have no reason to lie—if anything they have reason to simply go underground with these experiences, given the abuse they encounter from most outsiders when recounting *anything* about their lives.

As for myself, I believe that by recounting similar experiences of my own, expressing them as best as I can in English, and placing them in a much broader context, it might engender more understanding and respect on the part of those sceptics who are at least willing to listen. But I know one response is coming for sure: "Well, I can't explain it, but someday science will." But, as we've seen, Aborigines think "logico-deductively" and experimentally—it's just that they didn't apply this mode of thought to increasing their techno-environmental efficiency so that they could become independent of their neighbours before blowing them away when they became overpopulated or ran out of resources.

Crossing Over

"Crossing over" is based on the ability to connect the Amawurrena of one's *amugwa* (vital spirit) on "this side" to the Amawurrena of *awarrawalya* of something else on "this side" or on the "other side." This is by connecting to the "bits and pieces" of the "stuff of original creation" one has left behind or "rubbed off" on people or things as they proceeded through life. This connection is activated by Song—voice and *yiraga* (didjeridu)—performed separately or in combination. I'll begin with the *yiraga*.

Before it is "pulled" in performance (a reference to the role of the diaphragm in the exercise), the *yiraga* is (or used to be) empowered by smoking it. To demonstrate this, during a visit in 1993 Gula cut a special one for me from the bush, shaved it down to produce a B-flat on the fundamental (the preference here and purported to be the pitch of rushing water), and painted it with ochre in our Angalya's colours (red and yellow), then smoked it while chanting in the "Amawurrena of *awar-rawalya*" of important places nearby.

Pow pow, pow pow, pow, Milya:gburra,
Pow pow, pow pow, pow, Amalyu:a,
Pow pow, pow pow, pow, Amaugwara,
Pow pow, pow pow, pow, Mungwurridjira,
Pow pow, pow pow, pow, A:nemurremadja

Not all the Amawurrena of *awarrawalya* of the places sung into a *yiraga* are from the player's own Angalya—for example, none of the above (in retrospect, I think Gula's idea here was to keep me connected to Bickerton when I played back home). More often than not the player will perform for someone in another Angalya than his own and it helps if he is "tuned" to their Angalya. This arrangement is due to complex "boss/worker" relationships whereby one "works" or performs one's own Song but is "bossed" or overseen by someone in another Angalya, normally one eligible for marriage. So, "worker" sings, "boss" accompanies.

Smoking a *yiraga* in this manner helps channel the player's *amugwa* on his breath from the *yiraga* to the Amawurrena of *awarrawalya* of the places sung into it on the "other side" as he plays in uninterrupted fashion utilizing the technique of circular breathing (in and out at the same time). The Songman or woman follows, channeling his or her own *amugwa* on his or her breath with the Song and connecting to places on the "other side" in the same manner.

Men and women both sing and men take the lead, but only men pull the *yiraga*. Rather than illustrating a gender imbalance this seems to be an effort by men to balance the spiritual scales with women who alone enjoy a natural portal to the "other side." (This is a rule ruthlessly enforced by Aboriginal women whom I have seen snatch didjeridus away from European women trying to play them in the tourist traps of Darwin.)

Performances occur almost exclusively during mortuary ceremonies when the Song men and women of the Angalya of the deceased gather together (apart, of course, each in his or own small Song-space) to assist the *amugwa* of the person on its way. At this stage, his or her *amugwa* appears in translucent form, still somewhat humanly recognizable, but then gradually vanishes into its own reflected Essence of Being or *No*thingness after the Songmen and women release it to the "other side."

This is how Galiwaya Wurramarrba represented the (gender neutral) *amugwa* as such to me 50 years ago, in turn a representation of the carving shown to the initiates of his Angalya.

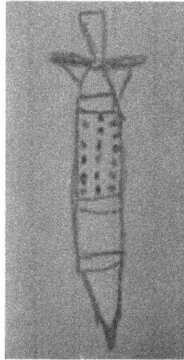

An abstract Form carved in wood hinting of human features, the infilling representing the Amawurrena of . . . will have to do.

The initial task accomplished of helping the *amugwa* of the departed on its way, members of the Angalya gather together again to burn the possessions of the departed, thereby releasing from them the "bits and pieces," the Amawurrena of *awarrawalya,* the deceased has left behind of himself or herself so that they can cross over to join him or her on the "other side." Bearing witness to this part of the ceremony are the *amugwa*-Essences of departed members of the Angalya who are sung to the edge of "this side" for the purpose. Again, the connection is made between those on "this side" and these on the "other side" through what remains of the "bits and pieces" of them that have been left behind during their lifetimes. (This is arranged by the living as a lock of hair and the bones of the deceased will be placed in a cave in the person's country in a few years' time so that a part of everyone is quite literally "here" forever.)

The early missionaries reported hearing such a constant stream of music in the camp night-after-night when they first arrived that they assumed these were a fun-loving people having a good time. In fact, it was the opposite. After the possessions of the deceased are burned the performers turn to the months' long task of visiting all the places the deceased has visited during his or her lifetime in order to gather up his or her Amawurrena of *awarrawalya,* or "stuff," and send it over to join him or her. This was before the advent of Europeans with mechanized means of transportation enabling Aboriginal people to travel much further afield. The alternative then was for the Songmen and women to stay put and let their *amugwa* do the traveling to these places to do the mopping up. This puzzled me no end when I first arrived, them sitting here while actually singing about being somewhere else!

So, rather than having a good time, what the early missionaries were witnessing with all the singing was people dispelling their grief. This was the only occasion on which people played before Europeans arrived and was still the custom when I first set down there. Playing for show was actually forced on them in 1969 by government officials when the entertainer Rolph Harris arrived for a visit and was followed by Alice Moyle, commissioned to record song and dances by the Australian Institute of Aboriginal Studies. Aborigines, being the accommodating people that they are, decided to comply but by secularizing the songs and dances, that is, by performing them at a "Dick and Jane see Spot run" level.

*   *   *

By 1995 I had learned to play the *yiraga* and my ambition was to play with Gula. So, come the dry season I made my way back to Groote and Bickerton. The problem was that Gula had "given up his tapping sticks" or retired from singing in ceremonies. This was a bit of a let-down, as I thought my chance had passed, but I was going to go see him anyway.

Gula greeted me on Bickerton with the usual "no money for food" and "no fuel for vehicle to get bush food," so I opened up my wallet and gave him half of what I had—about $20—and we went to the shop. Then, for no reason (but feeling a sudden flush), I opened up my wallet again and gave him the rest of my money.

I had almost committed a serious faux pas!

It was the Law that if someone asked you for something they needed and you had it, you must give *all* of it to them—not half, not a third, all!

This was taught to me during my initiation into the Warnungamadada during a mortuary ceremony in 1986 (recounted in *Return to Eden: A Journey through the Aboriginal Promised Landscape of Amagalyuagba*, revised and extended [Peter Lang Publishing, 1996]), my question then being, why had I not grasped it much earlier—17 years-and-up earlier? The reason is that I was blinded by the assumption that the transactions I was observing in their world were the same kind of transactions I was used to experiencing in my own. I mean who among us gives *all* of something they have to someone simply because they are in need of it?

Of course, once I was aware of this extreme act of charity, I saw it everywhere, noting now that when we went spear-fishing and someone came in with their catch they would give *all* of it up to those on shore, not just randomly but first to those who, in a sense, had least of nothing, namely the old people and children. I fell easily into line with this law, except for the occasional lapse such as with Gula above. But, then, sometimes, so did he, well, almost. . . .

Supplies at Milya:gburra were scanty—no flour, frozen meat, or veggies—so we picked up some rice, tea, tinned food, smokes, and a couple of drinks at the shop and the money was all gone. On the way back to his place Gula suddenly stopped and asked me, "Did you bring any food from Angurugu on Groote Eylandt for you and Nancy" (Damadada, named on The Sound of the Wings of the Curlew When It Flies, his *dadiyawa*—in our terms his "daughter," but much more and less in his,[2] who had come with me)?

"No," I said, "and I gave you all my money."

A worried look spread over *his* face and he reached into his pocket, fumbled about, and drew out the change left over from his purchases.

"Take this and buy something for you and Nancy for tea," he said. Not much, but it was *all* he had.

He later returned with a large portion of dugong meat. And . . . he offered to sing with me!

I had brought a *yiraga* with me—a ceremonial one given to me by Giningai Ngalmi (an Angalya we are connected to by Song on the mainland), a week earlier—and had found time to practice. Geraldine, one of

2. By this I mean that Aboriginal relationship terms mean much more or less than the simple individual kinship or genealogical connections ours refer to by including reference to the Angalya, or connections within the Angalya (the "more"), within a more generalized definition of paternity and maternity (the "less" aspect). Here, for example, a minimalist definition of *dadingyerga*, or wife, would be "someone in my father's mother's Angalya in my generation whose father's mother is in my Angalya." This is following the preferred situation in which a man/woman in one Angalya has married a woman/man from the same Angalya in the second generation—with the qualification that they are not marrying as "units" but as persons with individual, but very closely-related, Song identities. The aim is to match these, husband's to wife's, every second generation.

Gula's wives, was puzzled as to how I had learned to play the *yiraga*, and how I was allowed to play with Gula. Gula said I had been painted up in the ceremony and therefore could do so, and that I had learned to play by listening to the singing in the ceremonies all these years.

We settled in on his verandah as Gula began to shift himself into his Songspace by quietly singing to himself. After rehearsing briefly (below), we began, first on Duwalya, Curlew, with *degul degul* tonguing on the *yiraga*. These are the mouth sounds the "puller" makes to establish the appropriate rhythm, and in addition to this one there are two other basics: degula degula and degul degulagula. They are tonguing exercises and lead to more complex combinations until you become so adept you don't need them at all. (I was told about Djowila Nundirribala from Numbulwar on the adjacent mainland, who didn't even need a *yiraga*. He could "pull" from deep down inside himself employing his mouth cavity. Really! I caught him at the airstrip one day about to board a plane for home where he gave me a demonstration. Amazing.)

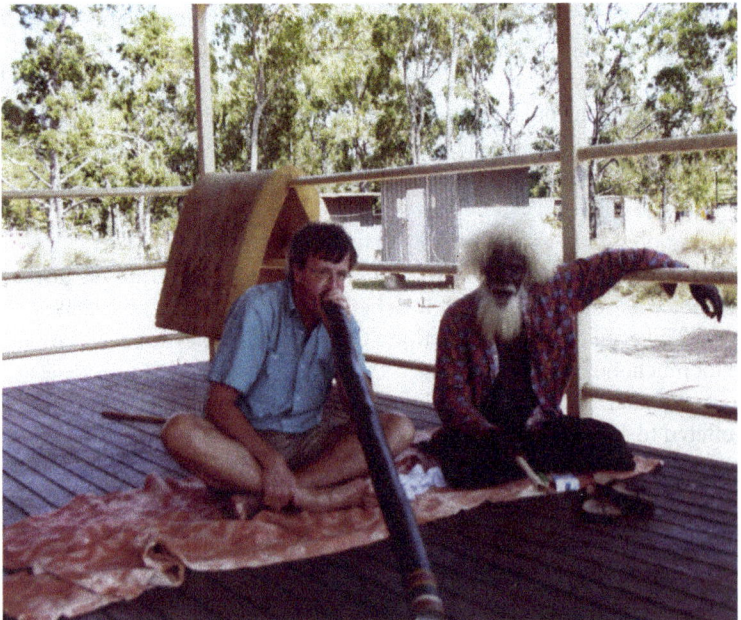

At first I was hesitant and a bit nervous but Gula kept going and it was up to me to maintain my rhythm in concert with the beat of his tapping sticks (thankfully for me at this point, a simple 1:1 ratio). We paused from time to time as the episodes in the Song were fairly short, and, as

I became more and more relaxed as we continued, I began to have this sensation of floating.

'Then, suddenly, the shape of the sound was clearly visible before me and I was soaring above the landScape, sectioned fields in illuminated outline below. I was aware of where I was. It was a mid-summer day over the countryside moving along the Scotch Line toward Perth. Clouds were imprinted in dark patches on the ground below. I was where most of my own "spiritual stuff" was—the place in Canada where I had grown up, to where I always returned, where my mother still lived, and where my father, my brother, and two sons were buried. The moment I realized where I was, the experience stopped and I was back playing with Gula.

Looking forward to playing with Gula I had imagined that my playing might take me on a spiritual journey to the "other side" with him through the Aboriginal landScape of Amagalyuagba following the journey recounted in of one of Gula's Songs—like Curlew. How naive of me. If I was going to cross over I would go where most of my own spiritual "stuff" resided, not theirs. I had no spiritual connection to any of the Warnungamada's Songs (for instance, those encapsulated within the term "Lalara," or Dangerous Snakes, and there were a lot of them at Amadadi on the adjacent mainland). I was Garuma ("little old wise man") to Gula's "the Professor" (just to keep things in perspective)—no Aboriginal name had been sung to me, that is, one with an Essence of Being. This honour Gula had intended to bestow on our son Iain had he survived cancer and returned after our visit in 1986.

But did I cross over? Well, partly: all I can say is, I "bore witness."

The experience was at least consistent with the fact that my *yiraga* had not been smoked (a practice now discontinued according to Gula) and had only my own spiritual "stuff" inside.

This was a level 4 experience. At level 5 I would not have returned. But it was confirmation that I was something more than just my physical self. I was an internally differentiated II: a part of "me" had departed (*antithesis*), returned to my material self (*thesis*), to "be" in relation to others (*plurality*).

*   *   *

I cannot recount a similar experience with singing because I do not sing. But Gula does and I can tell you what he told Nancy which convinced her beyond a shadow of a doubt—or perhaps in this context, "within a shadow of affirmation"— of the truth of what I have been relating.

Nancy had married Grant, a teacher at the Angurugu school, and moved south with him more than a decade ago to teach in New South Wales. Now Gula wanted her to return. So in 1993 he commissioned me to deliver this message to her, which I did on my return journey to Sydney before going home.

Two years later I was back and so was she. By now, though, having lived amongst non-Aboriginal Australians she was sceptical of the truth of the kinds of experiences I have related here. I mean, really, you're not going to get any kind of reinforcement for these in a small town in New South Wales. Well, one day, she said, her father told her he was going to Numbulwar on the adjacent mainland that evening to speak to some elders about a ceremony that was coming up and then coming straight back. She didn't know how he was going to do this as it was 87 kilometres (54 miles) across open water and there was no boat, no plane, and he couldn't phone as the only one available was locked up in the council office. Same in Numbulwar. No, he said, he was going to do it "Aboriginal way"— paint up, go into the bush, and sing himself over. This she did not believe.

So very early the next morning she went over to his hut and there he still was. She assumed he didn't go. But he said he had and proceeded to relate the conversation he had with certain Aborigines there whom he named. Sceptical, Nancy waited until the council office opened, went in and phoned Numbulwar asking to speak to one of the men he had mentioned. He came to the phone, told the same story as Gula about painting up and going into the bush, and recounted the conversation "word for word," she said, that Gula had related. After that she was a believer and grew to be a force in the community whose ambition was to lead in the singing which, she said, had been the custom in "olden times." Unfortunately she died a few years ago without quite achieving this goal.

If this kind of connection can be forged and activated between particular human beings—connectedness through their inter-connected Amawurrena of *awarrawalya*—then what about between particular human beings and animals? The problem here is that you would have to interact with a *particular* animal over a significant amount of time in order for the Amawurrena of your *awarrawalya* and theirs to "rub off" on each other and make a significant connection. That's generally not possible on an everyday basis. Individual animals are fleeting, particular ones just come and go more or less randomly. A pet might work but the Aborigines, at least, don't keep them. But a Vision Quest, as practiced in Canadian First Nations and Inuit societies, might, where the initiate is sent alone into the wilderness to make intense, intimate, contact with a particular animal as Piona Keyuakjuk recounts in *Eye of the Shaman*

(Rock's Mills Press, 2018). But as far as I am aware, Aborigines don't employ Vision Quests.

In the human scheme of things, Gula's "conference call" is one thing, utilizing these Amawurrena of *awarrawalya* connections to inflict harm on others is another. We call it sorcery. I witnessed the first act of it on Groote Eylandt in 1969 in the form of divination where a specialist from Ngukurr on the mainland was brought over to Groote Eylandt to locate the "killer" of an important ceremonial leader who had just died for no apparent reason as far as the Aborigines could tell. Without going into the details of what happened, the "killer" was to be located by the same means as he or she had used to "kill," that is, by connecting to the bits-and-pieces (of what remained behind of) the deceased's *amugwa* to the killer's *amugwa* and then removing it from the killer's body. Without it for some period of time he or she would "burn up with fever" and also die. Evil, or intrinsic "badness," is only curable by exorcism or death; badness is curable by rehabilitation, by all accounts the pre-contact Aboriginal way and into the post-contact period. The concept of evil came with the Christian missionaries.

On the other hand, these kinds of connections could be utilized for healing purposes, though I didn't encounter this in any of my visits. Perhaps those with this knowledge had gone underground, being in competition with introduced medical practitioners, one of whom, by the way, misdiagnosed what was septicaemia as a virus and almost left me to die on one of my visits. Thanks to Philippe Rouja who was assisting me at the time, I didn't.

Collapsing Time

When Frédéric Laugrand and his crew arrived from Laval University in Québec in the fall of 2016 to shoot a video for his series on Canadian anthropologists (http://www.anthropologie-societes.ant.ulaval.ca/les-possedes-et-leurs-mondes) I had just seen Denis Villeneuve's film *Arrival* with my son Liam and that's where I began. The main character of the film is a linguist and its main theme is her problems trying to decipher the language of the inhabitants of a spacecraft that has just landed, or at least hovered just above the ground. It's not a verbal language like ours with letters and words, but rather consists of swirls of smoke and plasma encoded with meaning.

In the film it's not clear when you are in the present or in the future. Or is it the past? The linguist appears to have lost a child and you think watching the film that it's already happened. But it hasn't. It's in the future. It's not time travel—it's the obliteration of time. As I said to Frédéric when the interview began, "If you think of yourself right now and you think back to when you came in the door, you can interpret that as, you came in the door, you sat down, and you began the interview. But what you've done is imposed time on what's actually a continual present." Each moment occurred in the "now." All you actually experience in life is a continual "now," right through from beginning to the end.

Something about *you* is in that continual present—or, that continual present is in *you*. If you reflect on it, something about yourself is always the same no matter what time in your life you are thinking about it. You just always know who "you" are. It's without time—or time is without you. In a sense, then, there's no past, no future, there's just this constant present that just keeps on going, and in the Aboriginal world it keeps going in this continual present after you die, but in another dimension, and you're there as "you," but in a different Form.

If all this is true, can you access this continual present which you've already experienced? And can you access this continual present which you've yet to experience? Because in this continual present there is no future, there is no past, just a continual now? This raised the whole issue for me of remembering accurately things that happened, say, 50 years ago. And it brought me to Gula and something that happened on Bickerton (by our calendar) in 1993.

Between 1969 and 1974, but mainly in 1969, I recorded 662 mortuary Songs during ceremonies at Angurugu and Umbakumba (an Aboriginal community on the eastern coast of Groote Eylandt). Some I had translated in the field, others for my Ph.D. thesis and for other publications, but most remained untouched (the politics of getting back to Groote Eylandt during this period is a whole other story). It was now almost 25 years later and I knew I had to at least get these Songs identified if not translated. They embodied the identities of the people who sung them and many of the Song men and women on my tapes had passed away. Though sung in public at mortuary ceremonies with words that identified the various Essences of Beings they represented, such as Curlew or Stingray, they also had hidden meanings know only known to the Songman or woman, as I discussed above.

Making the rounds back and forth between Angurugu and Umbakumba to find surviving Song men or women or their successors on the tapes who could identify their forebears' Songs required more time than I had available, so I decided to play a hunch and solicit Gula. He had for a very long time been regarded as the leading Songman in the region, able to sing multiple Songs at the same "time," switching back and forth between them during mortuary ceremonies. One potential difficulty was that the excerpts on my tapes normally lasted for only a minute or so, if that. Another was that I didn't know if he would know their hidden meanings as well as the public ones. I would have to assume at least the latter. To understand the former was something even he shouldn't know.

Gula agreed. He was living at Milya:gburra outstation on Bickerton.

We would follow the same procedure each day. I would rise at dawn and sit outside my *dongga* (pre-fab shed) having my cup of tea. Gula would then move out from his hut and sit in an open space facing me. This would last for about half-an-hour. Then he would get up and come over, sit down and, with a simple "turn on the tape," our work would begin. He had given instructions that no one was to approach while us we were working. The reason was simple. We weren't there, or at least he wasn't. Then, again, maybe I wasn't either from his perspective. We were back at the mortuary ceremonies recorded on the tapes.

Gula later told me that he sung himself over to me every morning and I noticed that he arrived with the same look in his eyes that the old people had when they sang during ceremonies—a kind of cloudy blankness that looked right through you to something behind you.

Gula's "memory" was phenomenal. He could say exactly who was there on the day a Song was being sung, the kind of day it was, where everyone was seated, including me, the conversations people were having. He could identify the Song, the Songman, and the *yiraga* player virtually the moment the excerpt began playing. One Song had but one note of the *yiraga* accompanying it. No problem.

Gula's so-called "memory" wasn't memory in our sense. His was an ability to access a dimension in which his own present coexisted with his past-present on the tapes such that he was in a position to "see" what was happening. He called this "seeing with my brain" (lit. *arrengemangma*). This is like looking at something with your eyes while you are seeing something else equally alive playing in your mind—sight, sound, everything. Weird sensation. How could he do this? It had to be via the Song with which he sung himself over to me every morning. I should have asked him what he had sung, but I didn't. My take on it is this: with his breath he projected his *amugwa* to connect via the Song to the "Amawurrena of *awarrawalya*," or "stuff of original creation," of himself, the place, and of those who were there at the time we were "remembering."

III. OUT OF TIME

The world of first Australians is a world transcending the dialectic of individual autonomy vs. collective unity based on a penetrating vision of reality that perceives the interdependence of all things as the basis of the make-up of the Cosmos and constructs its institutions accordingly. With personal identities founded on the notion of Song, the Aborigines escaped the pitfalls of seeing us primarily as biological beings, a notion which, when thrust into the midst of the dialectic of individual autonomy vs. collective unity, spawned the horrors of genocide on one plane and inherited privilege on another. You could travel anywhere in Aboriginal Australia with your Song and find connections through it to someone else's to establish a relationship. In fact, in principle, anywhere globally if this became a universal designation. After all, everywhere on the planet birds fly, fish swim, animals roam. If you can't connect there, then there's the sun, the moon, the stars. If language is a problem you can draw, and if that fails you can point. It's brilliant.

In a sense, the first Australians have been out of time, or rather out of *our* time with all its upheavals and missteps. Now, we in our time are almost out of time in a different sense unless we make some radical changes in relation to each other and the planet. We are masters at objectifying other people's beliefs but not our own. Objectifying is to dehumanize, to dehumanize is to discard. Doing so in the name of science doesn't make it right. This is a civilization that has endured for at least 70,000 years and must have done something right for some reason, or perhaps some reason beyond reason, seeing signs of the Eternal around them and, as Professor Berndt would say, "acting upon them."

We have lost touch with the planet. We pillage rather than nurture. Those with acute perceptual ability, able to see deeper into the nature of the world around us, we compartmentalize into the category "artists," assuming some biochemical difference from the rest of us. Their works enter the provenance of the rich or are collected up for limited public display in confined spaces such as galleries. We develop technology that separates us spatially from one another rather than connects us in a direct sense, mitigating the humanizing, connecting, effects of those bits-and-pieces of ourselves—the Amawurrena of original creation—the Aborigines identified within and around us all. And the further we march in this direction the greater the risk of self-destruction.

Heed the World of the first Australians. It's not that we have nothing to lose, so much as Nothing to gain.

Remembering Galiyawa

Darraragugwa, Peaceful Dove

P.S. Sitting in the camp with Galiyawa, July 20, 1969, radio turned to the moon landing, Galiyawa carving his spear. He listens but doesn't understand English. So he asks me what's happening. All I can do is point upward and say "*Na:nunggwarba, nawlegarna yimawura aeropla:na mandja da!*" (a man, he's travelling to the moon in an aeroplane). Galiyawa replies "*A:bina augwungwa langwa?*" (any water there). "*Nara*" (no) I reply. "*A:bina anenga?*" (any food). "*Narra*" again. "*Awurrariya angyalya*" (rubbish place), and he goes back to carving his spear.

IV. SOME PRINCIPLES TO LIVE BY

1. *Be respectful and friendly to everyone you encounter in life irrespective of race (colour), creed, or gender, recognizing that binary categories no longer apply.* You are "cosmologically" a part of one another and to disrespect someone on the basis that you are *not*, is to disrespect yourself. Apply the same principle to life in the natural world.

2. *Develop your visual, auditory, and sensual acuities (through the arts, contemplation, meditation).* "See" things for what they really are (or Not what they really are), instead of what someone tells you they are.

3. *In addition to your genealogical identity connect to the Essence of Being of something significant you have encountered in Nature.* We simulate this when it comes to labelling our political jurisdictions and sports teams: Ontario's Loon, Western Australia's Black Swan, the Toronto Blue Jays, the Collingwood Magpies (AFL), the Perth Blue Wings, Smiths Falls Bears.

4. *Be a giver not a taker,* being generous to others who have not, following the principle: If you have something someone needs (and you do not need it—a concession to our world), then make it available to them if they make that need known.

5. *Develop an "abundance" of something within yourself as a skill or service so as to provide it to someone who does not have it.* Then be the best at it you can be.

6. *Differences in kind (Indigenous, for instance) are to be enshrined politically with the proviso that they are also for the benefit of others elsewhere, not only those who embody them.* The latter would apply to basically *any* kind of difference that does not threaten to undermine someone else's difference.

7. *Support institutions that follow principles #4 and #5.* Profit is fine, excessive profiteering is not. Small and interdependent is beautiful, big and all-in-one boxes are not. Governance from the bottom up is fine, from the top down is not. Focus on your status as a citizen rather than a resident, ideally establishing it at a more local level.

8. *To be taken advantage of practicing principles #4 and #5 should not be tolerated and if it persists must result in the severing of all contact with the perpetrator.* The same principle applies to "legal persons" organized as corporations. Failure to do so will lead you to frustration, despair, and finally, anger.

9. *Partner in life with someone who follows principles #4 and #5 and avoid someone who follows #8.* Love is the ability to give of yourself at the most intimate level, anything less is unacceptable.

10. *Avoid the pitfalls of individualism on the one hand and collectivism on the other, particularly when pursued in separate streams of ideological fervour.* These are the ways of the dialect of violence and tyranny.

This takes us back to #1.

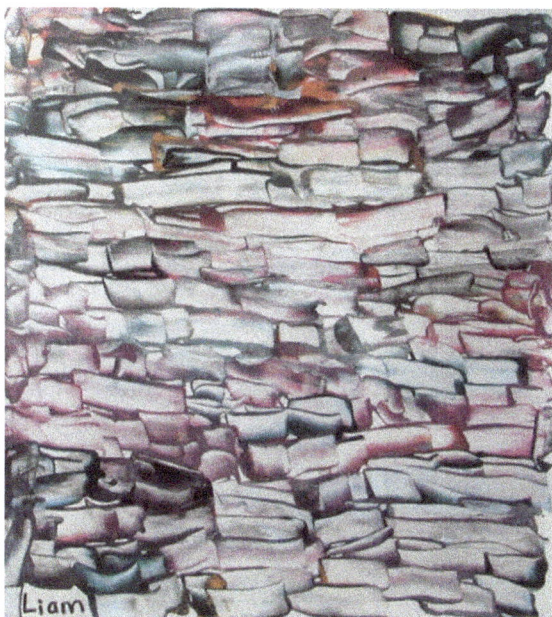

"Multiplicity," Liam Turner-Ponomareff, Grade 7